MW01233428

HABITS FOR

SUCCESS

Optimize Your Mind, Boost Your Productivity & Change Your Life

by FRANK J. OLIVER

Congratulation on purchase this book and thank You for doing so.

Please enjoy*!*

Table of Contents

INTRODUCTION

What we say and what we do. It affects how we feel physically, mentally and spiritually and it largely affects how successful we are in achieving our purpose and goals in life.

"Our attitudes control our lives. Attitudes are a secret power working twenty-four hours a day, for good or bad. It is of paramount importance that we know how to harness and control this great force." - **Tom Blandi**

Not everyone accepts or believes in positive thinking. Some consider the subject as just nonsense, and others scoff at people who believe and accept it.

It is quite common to hear people say: "Think positive!" to someone who feels down and worried.

Most people do not take these words seriously, as they don't know what it really means, or they don't consider it as useful and effective. How many people do YOU know that ever stop to think what the power of positive thinking can do?

To me, a positive thinker sees the bright side of life. Positive thinking is a state of mind, which focuses on the full half of the glass and not on the empty half. It is a mental attitude that expects positive results.

Let's take a look from the business perspective...

When you have a positive attitude and use positive language like, "I can save money," "I can lose weight," "I can reach my profit goals," then it just makes you feel better. You certainly feel better than you would if you spent the whole day focusing on what you can't do. And it's been proven that when we believe (or act like we believe) something to be true, it has a better chance of coming true. If we believe, for example, that we can lose 50 pounds, we can lose 50 pounds. The mind is a very powerful thing and our thoughts and the language we use affect our beliefs, actions and even our abilities.

Maintaining a positive attitude for business works the same way. It works whether you use it on yourself or to bolster others. You are going to be much more effective telling your sales agent to "go win that contract like I know you can" then to say to them, "don't you lose that contract!"

When you say, "don't you lose that contract" the image that one is left with is one of a contract being lost. Isn't that what you picture when you make that statement? It paints a negative image because it is a negative statement. Practice turning negative statements into positive ones. You end up saying the same thing, yet you paint a better picture and will thus get a better result.

Cultivating a positive attitude for business helps you get over challenges without even realizing it. When we have a positive attitude, challenges just seem to be less significant. It's not that positive people don't have challenges to overcome or get past; it's just that challenges have less of an effect on their life and their outlook than they do for negative people. If you have a negative attitude, the smallest setback can feel like Mount Everest. If, on the other hand, you have a positive attitude, even major setbacks feel do-able.

Creating a positive attitude for business helps you see opportunities rather than limitations. Opportunities, recognizing them and seizing them, is often the difference between tremendous success and just making a living. When you have a positive attitude, you view the world as a welcoming and friendly place and you expect, recognize and grab opportunities as they come to you. If you're negative then it's easy to view the world as your enemy and everything as a problem or limitation. Being positive makes a huge difference in your success.

A positive attitude for business also attracts people to you. It makes them want to do business with you and it brings opportunities, business partners, customers and friends to you. You're able to surround yourself with positive people and success easily.

Having a positive, can do attitude, gives you the extra edge to dream big and accomplish your goals. When you believe you can accomplish something, you're able to make it happen. You're able to sit down and plan how you're going to achieve your goals. You're able to focus on accomplishing the steps it takes to get where you want to go and you're able to celebrate and share your success with others.

What is the reason behind the different reactions from different people to one specific circumstance? Well, your reaction and ultimately your decision depend greatly on how you perceive a situation. Take a minute to view your mind and see the flow of your thoughts. Are those thoughts in your mind more of the negative ones or positive ones?

Have you ever wondered why a friend will walk up to you to cheer you up when you are feeling down even though you did not tell him or her anything about how you feel? It is not that your friend can read you like a book, but your attitude and expression tell it all.

So what actually that is so powerful to affect your attitude in general? It will be none other than your mind. If you are negative about certain things that happened, your powerful frame of mind will affect your attitude in general. You cannot simply hide your attitude as it will be shown through your face expressions, actions, speeches and appearances. Unless you are one excellent actor, people will sense your negativity when they come near you.

Beware! A negative mindset can be contagious. Anyone who gets near you can be affected by you almost instantaneously. Negativity will not only give you a gloomy and vexatious appearance, but also has the tendency to turn a happy gathering into a mourning session.

On the other hand, a positive mindset can energize you both mentally and physically, making you feeling more enthusiastic in pursuing your dream. Positivity has the power to make you appear happy and confidence. In addition, you can even have the power to affect others and hence, attract people towards you.

People with negative mind and hence negative attitude tend to shy away from challenges given to them. Negative thoughts may bring about fear; the fear of failure, the fear of what other would say about him or her, as well as the fear losing one's security. And when you are always in your comfort zone, you will never have the chance to step on the ground of a better zone.

A positive mindset and hence, a positive attitude can benefit a person a lot. A person who projects a positive attitude loves to take up challenges given to him or her. He or she is also better in handling pressure in life and is more proactive in solving problems. In fact, it was proven in studies that a positive mindset can even lead to better health.

If positive attitude gives such good benefits, why are most people around you seemed to have negative attitudes? You need to know that reality in life is not always everything's coming up roses and the worst fact is that there seems to be more negative things happening around you than the positive ones. Hence, unless you can be utterly oblivious of what is happening around you, you need to adopt a positive attitude to handle all these negativities and be a winner.

Nothing wrong to be feeling annoyed, down and sad at times, but to be in such stages for too long will not do you any good. In fact, these emotions can do harm to your health. Problems can arise no matter you are one positive guy or one negative soul, so why not adopt a positive attitude to solve your problems as it will make your life much easier. It won't do you harm and it has so much to gain just by believing in yourself. Start today.

CHANGE YOUR MINDSET – CHANGE YOUR LIFE

You know how can sometimes life can kick you in the crown jewels? Let's face it we've all had those days where everything that can go wrong does go wrong. Imagine this. You wake up late, you're late for a meeting, the PowerPoint presentation you prepared doesn't load so you do an ad-hoc presentation without any supporting materials and you get crucified by your bosses. You sit down at your terminal and then get called into the office for a 'performance review'. You're told you have 3 months to buck up or you're out of the door.

Ever felt like this and felt life is against you? Well it's time to get a grip. The really successful people in the world don't let any perceived setback ruin their day and they all progress towards their goals or aspirations.

If what you are doing now is not really what you want to be doing in the long term, ask yourself the reason you continue doing it.

For example if you have been doing a job which you don't particularly enjoy but by doing it you are acquiring skills you will need to have a job you really want, then there is a purpose.

But on the other hand if you are not enjoying your job and haven't explored other possibilities because you have made assumptions that there wouldn't be anything else suitable for you, then think again.

Perhaps you wanted to live in a certain place and be with certain people then the job might have been acceptable because it allowed you to do this. However in the long term, it's important to be more aware whether what you are doing is a choice or done for other reasons.

Even if it's not what you really want to be doing, there are changes in your approach you could initiate so that you begin to enjoy your job and life much more.

By changing your mindset about a situation you can stop or lessen the way some things become a great burden to you.

When you change your self-talk about what's going on you really can change the way you feel about it.

Instead of having a conversation with yourself or with others such as 'I never enjoy Monday afternoons' you could instead say something like ' Monday afternoons are always a bit of a challenge and I'm finding new ways to deal with those situations, by keeping calm, setting new boundaries and communicating more effectively.

It's strange but true that when you do things differently such as greeting people with a smile instead of a scowl or saying 'no' instead of 'yes' that other people will perceive you in a different light and will react in a new and, hopefully, more pleasant way to you.

Before any major change in our life happens, there must be a mindset change or upgrade. Our mindset controls our thoughts and what we believe is possible. The mind to the human is what the motherboard is to a computer. To run faster programs that require a lot of memory, we have to change the motherboard, to one with a bigger memory and faster processor. Trying to run a faster program on an old processor is a recipe for frustration.

As the old year recedes and the new looms in the horizon, there is a desire in every one of us for a better year, greater achievements, and moving to the next level. For this to happen in a sustainable basis, you have to upgrade your mindset. You have to change the way you think, what you see, and what you believe is possible. What you believe is real will ultimately become your reality. It is simply a matter of time. We create the future in our minds. If the future you see is more or less your present, then you have come to the end of the road.

Most companies promote staff, especially in the management cadre, based on their ability to function at the next level. No matter how good a supervisor you are, if you do not dress like a manager, walk like a manager, talk like a manager, function like a manager, you will not be promoted to the position of a manager. If anytime you act for the manager when he goes on vacation, everything falls apart, and the manager has to return to fix it, you will remain a supervisor for a long time to come.

If your desire is to end your career as a supervisor, then you have accomplished your dream, and can afford to settle. If you want to move on to become manager and beyond, then you have to move closer by upgrading your mindset to the managerial level. By the time the mindset upgrade is complete, you will begin to find yourself behaving like a manager in all ramifications. The change will be obvious to all. Your walk, talk, mannerism, confidence, knowledge etc. will change, and position you as manager in waiting. It is simply a matter of a manager's position becoming vacant. Rather than wait for longevity to come to your rescue (I ought to be promoted because I have spent donkey years in this position), you control the game by exhibiting the behaviors required for the next level. Instead of waiting for the ball to come to you, you contend for the ball and run with it.

The same applies to the game of life, and moving closer to your dreams. With a changed mindset, your thoughts change, your actions change, and a chain of events is set in motion culminating in the attainment of your set objectives. Your input changes, and inevitably, the output changes too. Insanity is also defined as doing the same thing over and over again, and expecting a different result. If you do not like the output you are getting, take a closer look at the input. Your mindset controls your input. If you believe something is outside your control, and all you can do is to wait for circumstances to come to your rescue, you will fold your hands, pray and do nothing to change the input. The moment you upgrade your mindset, and come to know that you can dictate the pace of the game, and ball control, you will think differently, act different (input), and get a different result.

If you've ever heard the saying - 'the power is in the conviction', then you'll understand my stand on mindset. I truly believe that we have the power to become anything and everything we desire. Of course all within reason. For instance, if you want to be an athlete, you must work very hard at the given sport and work beyond your threshold. Will that assure you of becoming an 'All-Star' or 'Professional Athlete'? Not sure, and I'd be lying if I gave you false promises, but I will tell you that you can be the best you want to be. Sometimes there will be limiting factors but that shouldn't stop you from trying to achieve greatness.

I am a people watcher and listener and because of this, I come across many who simply nail their feet to the ground before getting to the start line. With their negative thoughts or beliefs, they have already determined their outcome. Negative thoughts are extremely damaging not only to your psyche but to your overall health. Your mindset or your way of thinking will determine what paths your will take throughout your life. Notice how I mention, the word paths {plural} because after all we are human and will make mistakes or take a wrong turn. It is what we do after we have determined we have taken that wrong turn that separates the successful ones from the ones who simply stay on that chosen path.

So what can you do to change your mindset which in turn will change your outlook on life? Start off by determining what truly makes you happy. Write that on a piece of paper and work towards achieving that happiness. Yes, I said work! After all, we tend to appreciate it more when we work or earn it than if it is simply given to us. So, yes. Work towards your happiness and greatness. We all have our bad days, but again it will be up to you and your mindset, if you allow it to continue the entire day, evening and into the week. Try doing what I do, it may sound silly but it works. Every night before I go to sleep, I think of all the many blessings I had throughout the day from the breath I took to the smiles of my children. Then each morning I make sure to open my eyes, smile and again give thanks for all my many blessings and go on with my day.

So changing your way of thinking is not difficult but like anything that is worthwhile to accomplish, takes time to develop. Consequently, the teachings of a lifetime cannot be altered overnight.

But changing your mindset is what you must do in order to live the life you desire for yourself and your family.

By setting goals and working towards achieving them is the first step. By starting off small and increasing gradually you will find that your life will begin to have a new meaning. You will be able to see steady progress.

Once you have started reaching your goals then you should set more, all of the time putting in the hard work that it takes to meet your chosen goals. Monitoring and checking them each day to ensure you are making progress. The feeling you will experience when your initial minor goals are reached urges you on and you cannot wait to set more and work towards them, each time gaining momentum.

Eventually you will reach a stage where you ask yourself why you did not do this sooner. You are the only one who can answer that but from this point on, you only need to look to the future and the realization of how you can live the life that, once not so long ago, was only a dream.

The past is gone, put it behind you. It is time to move on and learn from the mistakes you made. You now need to be totally focused on your future and strive to achieve all that you desire and wish to attain.

In 'Rich Dad, Poor Dad' Robert Kiyosaki talks about what it takes to become a sophisticated investor. He states that you need be earning at least $200,000 a year, and then goes on to say that if you think that is a lot of money, you are right, it is, and it probably always will be to you. But, if you see that as an achievable goal to set yourself, you will get there. A large proportion of our lives are determined by the personal perception we have of ourselves, our values, our beliefs and our surroundings. If you want to live an above average life, then start by changing your mindset.

Changing your mindset involves the stubborn side of your attitude. You need to decide what you want to do or believe and refuse to believe anything else. You need to decide that $200,000 is not a lot of money and start exploring and studying ways for you to achieve your earnings goal, whether it is $100,000, or $1 million, or $100 million. If you get the chance Google 'Bill Bartman' and see the decisions he made to get to where he is today.

The bottom line is that it is up to you and only you to make a difference in your life. Don't worry about things out of your control, only focus on what you can control. Start with changing your mindset.

Change Your Habits - Transform Your Life

Watch your habits, for they become character. Watch your character, for it will become your destiny. Not your authentic destiny, but yourself made one. Bad habits can really disturb our destiny, from manifesting. Actually, many people have gone to their grave, with unfulfilled potentials, because of their bad habits. So as we can see, our bad habits go to go.

The problem is habits are almost automatic. So instead of choosing our best option, we tend to keep doing what we are used to them. And instead of stopping the habits, whenever we want, we are more likely to keep repeating the pattern, because of the controlling power of bad habit. But be rest assured, today you're going to learn 3 simple steps that are going to help you, control any habits, as opposed to them controlling us. And these simple steps are called: Causation, Formation and Transformation.

So the first simple step I'm going to talk about: Causation, The meaning of causation is identifying what caused something to happen. What I mean by causation is identifying the root cause of a habit. There is usually no smoke without a fire. Causation is identifying patterns that trigger the habit. For instance, in whose company does the habit usually occur, what kind of thoughts triggers the habit, and how often does the habit occur daily. This will empower us to kick the habit.

Following this further, Dr Phil once famously says, we can't change what we can't acknowledge. Let's face it, we all have bad habits. So to motivate ourselves to stop, ask yourself what your habits are stealing from you. Because habits are thieves, they can steal your time, your joy or your self-confidence, among other things. For instance, a habit of negative self-talk can steals confidence, a habit of unhealthy eating can steals a positive self-image, and a habit of laziness can steals future success.

In the same way, you didn't form your habits in a day, so don't expect to stop them in a day either. It's going to take some time, some effort, and consistency. But you know you are worth it. So acknowledge that you have a habit, and start working on it today. Invariably, kicking a habit is not easy, but keeping the habit will cost you more. It will cost you your joy, your wellbeing and your freedom.

So the second simple step I'm going to talk about: Transformation.

Transformation is becoming the improved version of yourself. But in order to transform yourself, you have to first change. But any change in life, without first changing the underlining bad habits, is just temporary. For instance, someone who has a low self-esteem, and had a plastic surgery in order to feel better, about themselves, will only feel better for a short while, until they find something else they want to change. This is because they are trying to fix an internal problem, like low self-esteem, with external measures. Without first changing the habitual pattern that led to a problem, the getting rid of the low self-esteem is just, will just temporary.

It easy to see that, if you want something to change in your life, the changing the underlying habit starts with you. I mean we can't keep doing the same thing, and expect a different result. 1+1 will always be 2. So, if we keep doing the same thing, we will always get the same result. But the good news is, research shows, it only takes 21 days to form a new habit, so start today.

On the other hand, our habits are usually triggered by what are called triggers. In fact, it is not life events that make you respond to life the way you do, but your triggers and your conditioning. For example, school children can be conditioned to being hungry by the school bell, shocking isn't it. The truth is, anytime they hear the school bell for lunch, whether they were hungry or not, they become hungry instantly. But when they can avoid the exposure to the bell, which is the trigger, let's say on school holidays, they would avoid the emotional hunger that the bell creates, after about 21 days of forming the new habit.

In the same way, identifying, avoiding and replacing any psychological triggers will empower us to kick the habit. This is known as positive feedback. Having said that, negative feedback can help you kick your habits, if it is your cup of tea. Negative feedback involves putting a rubber band on your wrist, so anytime you become tempted to do the habit, you snap the rubber band on your wrist. Ouch, I know which one I prefer. But seriously, negative feedback trains the mind to avoid a habit, in order to avoid the pain. But both negative and positive feedbacks work. And the choice is yours.

The third simple step I'm going to talk about: Formation.

Formation is act of forming something. But what I mean by formation is forming new good habits, to replace the bad ones, in order to change your life. Find something else to focus on to distract you from your habit. The devil uses idle hands. And our focus usually becomes our desire. Find something positive that will overshadow your habit, to desire. For example, someone who has a negative thinking habit, and decides to starve their negative thinking to death, with positive self-talk. This will starve their habit to death, and they will end up developing, a new positive mindset.

Moreover, find a new hobby that helps you to maximize your strengths or a new hobby that helps you to develop new strengths. For instance, learning to play music, learning to write or learning to paint, are good diversions from any bad habit. These kinds of hobbies are also therapeutic. Besides that, beware of what I call the comfort zone syndrome. Because every time you step out of familiar a ground, that is your comfort zone, You will develop some anxieties, due to fear of the unknown. All you need to do is to keep talking yourself out of the anxiety. Keep reminding yourself what have to gain, when you lose the habit. If you are consistent for about 21 days, you will lose the anxiety, and gain more confidence, about your ability to stay away from your unwanted habits.

So lastly, as Shaquille O'Neal famously said, you are what you repeatedly do. And I am saying to you, in order to become what you want, make a habit of doing only things that are becoming of you.

MASTER YOUR EMOTIONS – OPTIMIZE YOUR MIND

Life can be an extremely difficult journey. It's collection of movements are all the more critical, it seems, the longer we remain here. At times we get to the point where we're asking ourselves, "How will I make it?"

"This is too much, I give up!"

You must know what to do when things get unbearable to avoid the thought of calling it quits. Like anything else, knowing what to do takes practice. We will never receive the proper training without the confrontation of unwanted emotions.

After years of practice, you can learn to master all your emotions. It's easy to master and manage what is pleasant, but how about what isn't? When you want to begin to overcome and become a master of your unwanted emotions you have to first recognize them. Often people wait until it is too late.

The word emotion is derived from the Latin word meaning "to move out" or "to excite" and Psychologist define emotions as ' physiological changes and conscious feelings of pleasantness or unpleasantness aroused by external and internal stimuli that leads to behavioral reactions' (Davis and Palladio: Psychology 2nd ed.). Simply put your emotions are what you are feeling at any given moment no matter what is happening to you and it makes you react and behave in certain appropriate ways.

Many persons feel that their emotions are not in their control. They believe that they are slaves to their emotions and that they are just reacting to the events of their lives. There are even those who fear their emotions as if it is some great big tyrant. In an effort to avoid feeling certain emotions many people do things like turn to drugs, alcohol, overeating, sex and even get into a paralyzing depression.

How To Master Your Emotions

The first thing you need to do when mastering your emotions is to know your true feelings. Have you ever felt so overwhelmed that you don't even know what you're truly feeling? All you know is that negative emotions and feelings seem to be swarming through you. Interrupt this pattern by stepping back for a moment and just ask yourself "What am I truly feeling at this moment?" if your fist thought is that "I'm frustrated" ask yourself right away "Am I truly frustrated or is it something else?" "Could it be that what I am feeling is disappointment?" By simply taking a moment to figure out what you are truly feeling and questioning and challenging your emotions you will be able to lessen the intensity of the emotion you're experiencing and hence be able to deal with the situation much quicker. You'll also find it easier to learn from the emotion.

Next you must admit and give value to your emotions, because they anchor you. Many of us have had those moments when we make our emotions wrong. This is something you should never do, as it is a sure way of blocking true communication with your inner self and even with other persons. What you must do is be grateful and thankful that your brain is sending you signals of support urging you to take action to change your perceptions or something in your life even your present actions. By trusting your emotions even when you don't understand them and knowing that they are there to support you in making positive changes, you will begin to end the internal wars you have with yourself. You'll then begin to seek out and move towards the simpler solutions.

You then have to be eager to learn what your emotions are saying to you. Do not just accept your emotions on face value, for sometimes what you presently feel is really about something else. When you become eager to learn what your emotions are saying to you, you will begin to master them, which in turn assists you in solving the challenge and prevent the said problem from reoccurring. So if you find yourself feeling rejected, for example, ask yourself "could I be misinterpreting the situation to mean I'm not good enough, when in reality I am using one instance to make my determination?" "What if I approached other persons who may be accepting of me?" "Is my feeling rejected a message that I need to take action to change how I present myself? Ask yourself the following four questions when questioning what your emotions are saying to you:

1. What is it that I truly want to feel?
2. To feel the way I have been feeling what would I have to believe?
3. To create a solution and handle this right now what am I willing to do?

4. Is there anything I can learn from this?

5. What actions can I take now?

You answers to these questions will help you to learn about your emotions and their uniqueness each time they occur.

It's very important that you believe you can do it, that you can deal with this emotion right now. The simplest, most powerful and quickest way to handle an emotion is to recall an instance in the past when you felt a similar emotion and recognize that you had successfully handled it before. If you dealt with it in the past then it is possible that you can deal with it again right now. Think about how you dealt with your emotions in the past and use this as your guide for what you can do right now to change how you feel. What was your process back then? Did you change your perception, what you focused on, and the questions you asked yourself? Do the same things right now believing that it will work just as it did before. So if you're feeling lonely, for example, and you were able to turn it around in the past, ask yourself "What did I do back then?" Did you take action by calling up some of your friends and staying in touch with them thereafter? Did you visit your friends at their home? Whatever you did in the past try them out right now and you will likely get similar results.

Next you have to be sure you can handle the emotion in the future. To do this you need a great plan to do so. One method you can use is to remember the way you have handled it in the past and rehearse handling those situations where this negative emotion would come up in the future. You will have to use visualization to hear, feel and see yourself handling the situation with ease. By doing this over and over again with some emotional intensity will cause your behavior to be set in such a way you will easily deal with the challenge. You can also write down a couple of other ways (at least four of them) you can change your perceptions when negative emotions arises. Do this also for ways you can change how you communicate your feelings and your needs and also for ways you could change the actions you were taking in this particular situation.

The next step is to take action. It makes no sense to go through the first five steps and not take immediate action, you would have wasted your time and nothing would have changed. So once you believe you can handle an emotion take action immediately to prove to yourself that you can handle it.

These six steps can help you master any emotion that may arise in your day-to-day life. Practice using these steps as often as you can it may seem hard at first but the more you do them the better and simpler it will become for you. It is important that you realize that the best time to deal with an emotion is when you first start feeling it. So don't delay in applying the six steps and save yourself the distress.

Abraham-Hicks Process, The Emotional Scale, And Hypnosis

The things that we learned from The Secret and the Law of Attraction is so fascinating. What is most appealing about these powerful teachings is how you don't have to struggle to get what you want and the Universe will deliver your desires. You just have to think positive thoughts.

One of the most prominent leaders of the Law of Attraction movement, Abraham-Hicks, has been creating a lot of positive impact on thousands of people all over the world.

The main focus of the Abe teachings is feeling good. When you feel good and stay there for as long as you can, you will allow all the things you've ever wanted into your physical reality much faster.

The skill to learn here is to feel good no matter what the circumstances are and when you master this, you can access unlimited happiness whenever you want. Achieving goals become a breeze and certain, not possible or probable but CERTAIN.

Instead of stressing yourself out on taking physical action, take mental action first which means thinking positive thoughts so you feel good.

Abraham calls this process a lot of things and they use several really powerful metaphors.

Example:

- Lining up your energy
- Aligning with the power that creates worlds
- Going with the stream
- Getting into the vortex

They also provide what is called the "Emotional Scale". Here it is:

EMOTIONAL SCALE:

1. Joy/Appreciation/Empowered/Freedom/Love
2. Passion
3. Enthusiasm/Eagerness/Happiness
4. Positive Expectation/Belief
5. Optimism
6. Hopefulness
7. Contentment
8. Boredom
9. Pessimism
10. Frustration/Irritation/Impatience
11. Overwhelment
12. Disappointment
13. Doubt
14. Worry
15. Blame
16. Discouragement
17. Anger
18. Revenge
19. Hatred/Rage

20. Jealousy

21. Insecurity/Guilt/Unworthiness

22. Fear/Grief/Depression/Despair/Powerlessness

With number 1 being the highest positive emotion and 22 being the lowest negative emotion, this list is a hierarchy of feelings. Let me give you an illustration of how the whole Abraham process works.

If you're feeling hatred or rage (number 19), you usually can't go up to the feeling of love (number 1) immediately because the vibrations, based on the scale, are so far apart. It'll be harder for you make that jump. So the best and logical step for you would be to go up the emotional scale step-by-step, piece-by-piece.

You have to manipulate and work your feelings to revenge (number 18) first. Now, it's still a very negative emotion (and please don't do anything hurtful to yourself or anyone) but you'll feel a little bit of relief since it feels better than getting caught up in rage.

As best you can, work yourself up to discouragement, then to blame, to worry, to doubt, to disappointment, to frustration, to pessimism, to boredom, to contentment, to hopefulness, to optimism, and high as you want to be.

The goal here is to feel good and if you can just get into the vibration of hopefulness (contentment is good too by the way), you'll feel much better and you also get to experience a big relief... seriously.

There are a lot of techniques in the Abe toolbox (the latest is the emotional grid process) and the good thing about this is you can choose any tool that will fit your current situation. I like the find a better feeling thought process, getting into the vortex, and filling your own emotional grid.

Eventually, I had a sudden realization. That those I've learned from Brian Tracy and others from the "work hard" school of thought can be easily blended with Abe's teachings. I finally meshed hard work with the ease and flow of the law of attraction. Abe said (as how I interpreted it) that you can work hard and apply any school of thought as long as... and this big one...

You feel good.

You can work as hard as you like, strive to be more productive as you like, you can do whatever you want as long you feel good. That's your key indicator. If a philosophy feels good and resonates with you, do it. That's all there is.

My advice is to take what you want from Abraham. Honestly, there are some things about the teachings that I personally disagree with but the tools I picked were effective for me.

You got to have your own philosophy in life or your own way of living. Be just like Bruce Lee... take what is useful and take what is useless.

BOOST YOUR PRODUCTIVITY

All successful people are very good time managers who can organize their life very well in all aspects. Very advanced time management will lead to productivity in your life just as those successful people have achieved.

The key to success is not a secret. I will try to share with you some of the basic hints on the way to become a more productive and successful person. Do not forget that what you gain from this material as a habit may change your life.

Productivity means the ability to create results. Most of the time, results are not borne without obstacles. Your latitude to solve problems will determine how productive you will become. Men that have their name imprinted on the sand of time are those who have overcome great obstacles and challenges in life. Benjamin Franklin said "All mankind is divided into three classes: those that are immovable, those that are movable and those that move."

Life is governed by principles and it takes those that understand these dynamics to break away from the crowd. There is always a popular opinion and there is the tendency to always want to flow with this but I have discovered over the years that those that have chosen (yes, it's a matter of choice) to stand out from the crowd to become outstanding in their chosen endeavor are people who have gone against popular opinions.

Thomas Edison, the inventor of the light bulb was told by his teacher that he was too stupid to learn anything.

Wilma Rudolph contracted polio at the age of four, she was told she would never walk again but she went ahead to become a runner and won three Olympic gold medals. She was known at a point to become the "fastest woman on earth."

Albert Einstein did not walk until the age of four nor could he read until he was nine-year old. He failed most of his college entrance exam and eventually went ahead to become one of the greatest scientists the world has ever known. I can go on and on to share with you more stories of those who went against the popular opinions and eventually went ahead to be the very best. God has given us all talents and gifts. You need to find what it is and just DO IT.

I am a firm believer that whatever the mind can conceive one can achieve. Find your gift or talent and just go for it. To be productive in life you must understand principles that govern productivity. There is the application of heuristics which are rules intended to help provide solution to problems. There are times when a problem is large or complex, and you are at loss of what steps to take; applying a heuristic lays the foundation for making progress towards a solution even though you can't visualize the final picture from the starting point. Below are principles that have helped me:

1) Bust Procrastination - Bury procrastination by doing that task NOW! Procrastination is a subtle enemy of productivity. It requires conscious effort to defeat it. Study for that exam now, register that business now, go for more training now... don't keep postponing. DO IT NOW! To defeat procrastination learn to tackle the most difficult tasks when you are unsullied and this is usually in the morning. When you succeed with this, you will succeed with every other.

2) Set goals - Without goals, life will be meaningless. Set daily goals for yourself. Make sure you understand in clear terms what your goals are. Set targets that are attainable. Know what you want to do and do it.

3) Clustering - Cluster similar tasks together and run through them in one piece. This will not give room for slog.

4) Focus - Set block of time where you can work singly without being interrupted. Whatever causes distractions must be put away during this period. It could be the internet, friends or other things that you can identify as distractions. It could sometimes require that you switch off your phones or other communication gadgets

5) Set Deadline - This helps you to stay on track and gives a time frame for your tasks. Imagine a football match without a time frame. Every football player knows they have ninety minutes to win the match hence they are being driven by that consciousness.

6) Employ Pareto - This is the 80/20 rule which means that in anything a few (20%) are vital while

many (80%) are trivial. Here is the take, the Pareto principle should serve as a daily reminder to focus 80% of your time and energy on the 20% of your work that is really important. Don't just work smart but do so on the right things.

7) Paint a Picture - Start out with having a clear picture of what your finished task will look like. Visualize the finished product from the start and tailor your plan to achieving success around this.

8) Relax - Don't make it all work and no play. Take time out in between tasks. Taking few minutes to relax the brain can help reduce the brain pressure and get you relaxed and refreshed to resume your task again with fresh vigor.

9) Feedback - Set up a mechanism that helps you to take stock. You do this by asking questions and finding answers in the goals you have set for yourself for that day, week, month or year. Based

on the system's response, set up task for the next day and move ahead.

10) Get Out - Opt out of friendships that will not add value to your life. Exit clubs and organization that consume your time more than they are worth. Quit programs that are an absolute waste of your time.

11) Draw Inspiration - You can draw inspiration by reading books of acclaimed authorities in various fields of life endeavors. Attend seminars and conferences that will add value to your life. Make God your ultimate source of inspiration because He is the endless reservoir of divine inspiration.

12) Keep Fit - It is difficult for a sick person to be productive. Exercise daily. Eat right. Enhance your physical and mental metabolism. Avoid unhealthy habits.

Plan your every days' actions in detail. Beginning planning for long period of time, complete your plans by detailing them with the shorter periods for sub-plans. For example, make a list of targets you are planning to achieve for the next year. Write every detail on a sheet of paper. Let your brain emits every single word telling your target. After planning your actions for the next year, develop sub-plans for the next months. Then do planning for the following weeks. Continue until you plan each day in the next few weeks. Do not forget that an advanced planning prevents undesired consequences.

THE MORNING HABIT OF SUCCESSFUL PEOPLE

It should be quite obvious that habits are one of your biggest assets when it comes to being successful. The people who are successful in this world are the people who developed the right habits. They don't have to think about doing things that make them successful. They just get up every morning and do them which of course give them the results that they want in the long run. create habits that will allow you to change your mindset from a negative self-destructive one to a healthy mindset that is ready for success.

We've all heard the old adage, "the early bird catches the worm." But the siren-like lure of the snooze button is just so hard to ignore. 10 more minutes, 10 more minutes. You hit snooze a few times and the next thing you know, its all-out morning mayhem—you barely have enough time to brush your teeth, never mind read a leisurely article in your favorite magazine while sipping on a freshly-brewed cup of dark roast.

I've seen it a million times. In fact, I've done it a million times.

But once I recognized the value of those early morning hours, I quickly changed my tune. Studies have shown that our willpower is strongest in the morning—it gets muddled by exhaustion and other priorities as the day goes on.

From working out to reading the news and meditating, your early morning hours are sacred time that can, and should, be spent doing things for yourself. Because once the workday begins, you hit the grind and by the end of the day, who knows if you'll have any time for yourself.

A majority of highly successful business executives, entrepreneurs, and celebrities wake up early so that they can make the most out of every minute of their day — especially their mornings. And most use this quiet time to prepare for the day ahead, get in the right mindset, and set a positive and productive tone for the day. So, instead of hitting that snooze button, it's time to take back your mornings.

Capitalize on sunrise and implement these 10 morning habits to improve your productivity and set yourself up for a successful day:

Wake Up Early

Do you know why most millionaires wake up early in the morning? Do you even know that wake up early in one of the most important factor in your life? Why it is not discussed more often anywhere else?

Wake up early in the morning gives you the following benefits:

80% of people who live longer than 75 years old is the person who wake up early.

Wake up early is helpful in training your determination and confidence. Both qualities are important for a successful person.

Wake up early will energize sensitivity, creativity and stability of a person.

Your efficiency and productivity in the early morning is 3 times higher than day time.

Wake up early will bring create a sense of optimism in your life. You will start enjoying changes of nature in a special way.

Some people find it really hard to be awake early in the morning every day. They feel so lazy to stand up and do the things that need to be done. You need to know that you have to learn on how to wake up early each time. You need to do this for your own good.

In order to accomplish the task of waking up early, you need to start your plan as soon as you could. Do not bother about what time you go to bed, but you need to set a clear goal of when you want to wake up the next morning. Treat this as the most important challenge you ever have in your life.

It is definitely not that easy to wake up from your sweet dream in the early morning. Is it possible to be accomplished? There is no right or wrong answer. It depends on whether you are willing to challenge yourself and take a positive step to enjoy early morning dawn.

You need to get rid of early morning sluggishness and laziness and jump out from your bed when you get the first signal of alertness. Do not procrastinate and lying on the bed any further.

Waking up as early as possible is the first step. It's not as hard as it seems. Once you accommodate this habit, it will feel pleasurable instead of painful. This doesn't mean cutting hours from your sleep. It means going to bed earlier than you usually do.

Most of us know that doctors suggest that the best hours of sleep are from 10 PM to 6-8 AM. Successful people know that time is priceless – and that's exactly why they tend to wake up extremely early. If they have a great start in the morning, they'll get more results and personal time.

Keep Your Room in Order, Make Your Bed

This one might not seem that important, but it is! This one-minute habit will help you start the day right and cut the temptation of going back to bed. You will be surprised to know that every successful person does this.

Furthermore, there is even a book called "The Power of Habit" by Charles Duhigg, that talks about how making your bed is a routine that significantly improves productivity.

Healthy Breakfast

Remember the speech "breakfast is the most important meal of the day" from you mom?

Your mom isn't the only expert in our midst. According to Mayo Clinic breakfast fuels the body and gives you energy to keep you going for hours. The National Institute for Health reports that when you eat a healthy breakfast you are less likely to overeat later in the day. Weight Watchers teaches if you are trying to lose weight - skipping meals may cause you to gain weight. Think about this. Breakfast is really "breaking" your night time "fast". So if you skip the first meal of the day your body will be running on the energy (food) from the day before. That's a lot to ask of your body. Don't you think?

Eating a healthy breakfast is one of the most important ingredients of living a healthy life. Unfortunately, however, many people hardly eat anything in the morning. I admit I was that way too occasionally when I was still in school. It mostly happened when I was cramming for an exam the night before; I would then want to get an extra hour of sleep instead of eating breakfast.

I know a few people who started forming the unhealthy habit in school which later got carried into their adult lives. They are so used to not eating in the morning that they don't even feel hungry until lunch time. So they tend to eat a big lunch and again a big dinner in the evening. This is a way for your body to make up for not getting a healthy breakfast when you rise. You may not feel any negative effects from it until you get older and your metabolism slows down; you then start to gain weight and have a lot of health issues associated with it like high blood pressure and cholesterol, diabetes, etc.

On a side note: do NOT bring breakfast to work! You might feel stressed or hurried, so you might make a mess and give yourself extra work. Also, don't forget about drinking enough water throughout the day!

Keep Your Body Hydrated

The human body is made of 75 percent water, so you can see why drinking at least 2L every day is so important and healthy. Moreover, drinking water on an empty stomach is one of the best morning habits to adopt. Successful people always keep their bodies hydrated in order to have more energy throughout the day.

It is important for everyone to know at least the key benefits of hydration in order to live a healthy life. Hydration assists the body to keep its temperature normal. It helps body organs to work efficient and absorb the nutrients and to change the food into energy. Drinking water is also essential in removing the waste from body. It helps to moisturize oxygen that we take in, and circulate the blood in every part of the body. Water makes seventy five percent of our brain, which means that by drinking water we will not suffer a headache. It is beneficial for bones, muscles and helps to remove waste materials from body.

Tips:
Hydration matters for all whether they are at home or at work or playing sports. Sometimes people do not realize that they have missed drinking water or any other liquid after sports or exercise. An important tip is to drink any liquid during day after

every 15 minutes, also before starting exercise or any sports. Drinking water is necessary in order to avoid dehydration in a quantity of two cups and two cups after the exercise.

Workout Routine

The following is an excerpt from "What The Most Successful People Do before Breakfast" by Laura Vanderkam:

Perusing the Wall Street Journal over coffee the other morning, I learned that while I was still sleeping, Reverend Al Sharpton had already done a workout. "He has a gym in his Upper West Side apartment building, where he's usually the only one working out when he arrives around 6:00 am," the paper noted.

He warms up for ten minutes on a stationary bike and jogs thirty minutes on a treadmill. Then it's on to the stability ball and crunches. "On days he can't get in his morning workout, he uses the gym at

NBC Studios. He travels to two to three cities per week and says he makes his staff call ahead to ensure the hotel has a gym."

Exercising in the wee hours, he never worries about what he looks like. "I usually wear an old track suit and Nikes," he told the WSJ. "It's so early no one sees me." Coupled with dietary changes, however, this early-morning ritual in grubby clothes has made the reverend look quite spiffy. He's lost more than one hundred pounds in the past few years.

"If it has to happen, then it has to happen first."

James Citrin, who co-leads the North American Board and CEO Practice at the headhunting firm Spencer Stuart, is also often exercising by 6:00 am. He uses that early-morning quiet to reflect on his most important priorities of the day.

One day a few years ago, he decided to ask various executives he admired about their morning routines for a Yahoo! Finance piece. Of the eighteen (of twenty) who responded, the latest any of them was up regularly was 6:00 am.

For instance, according to the interview notes Citrin later shared with me, Steve Reinemund, the former chairman and CEO of PepsiCo, was up at 5:00 am and running four miles on the treadmill. Then he had some quiet time, praying and reading and catching up on the news, before eating breakfast with his then-teenage twins.

You may be surprised how a little workout in the morning can change your mood over the day. Successful people understand the benefits of exercising. They know that it boosts energy, prevents high blood pressure, and releases endorphins that create feelings of happiness. As you exercise, you're also keeping your body fit and on top form.

Meditate

I will not claim to be fully recovered or a highly successful millionaire. But I can say that within a few days after I found the solution, I found myself a hundred times closer to my goals. What I found was, I am still able to meditate. Everyone is.

And here is another thing I found. All the success coaches - all those motivation guys who want to put you together with your destiny - they all know about the power of meditation. And most even talk about it in one way or another; they just never call it, "meditation."

You see, to make things click, to bring peace and harmony into your life, even to bring more money into your life, you don't even need to do the kind of meditation most people do. There's another easy kind of meditation that only takes about 20 minutes. At 20 minutes a day, a person can build up ability really fast.

Meditation, alone, cannot bring a person out of any mess he is in. It is not magic. However, sometimes the results of meditation feel magical, and meditation does help you get your head straight.

Recovery from years of loss will not happen in one day. But I do believe that meditating one time, the right way, can lead to giant leaps on the road to inner-peace, harmony, and success. I believe it can only do great things for you if you make it a daily habit.

I also believe, from experience, that meditation can help you bring about the changes in your life that you seek, but only if you don't depend on meditation to do it. What I mean is, the reason for meditation is NOT to bring changes in your life. But things occur in the meditative state that brings about changes that you want.

The reason for meditation is to relax your body and clear your mind. That is what you must intend when you meditate, nothing else. To clear your mind means just that - "clear." No goals, no problems, no anticipations, no disappointments, no tension, and no stress... Just a clear mind - ready to receive what comes your way.

Along with success comes a stressful life. Meditation is your chance to escape, even if it's only for a little while. Facing stress is not easy.

You'll need to handle it with calmness, so it won't control you. Through meditation, successful people find their way to keep their cool, to disconnect from their stressful life, and to clear their minds.

Plan The Day Ahead

It's important to fix your schedule from home. Once you know what you have to do, your mind is already prepared for what comes next and you can handle it with more ease.

Plus, the moment you arrive at your workplace, you can start working immediately so you won't lose any time. Successful people with morning habits use to-do lists in order to visualize their priorities and introduce small breaks, as nobody likes mental burn outs.

Make a candid review of what your current time frame really is. What are you doing for your work time, your family time, are you all over the place of do you have a set schedule?

Look for office hours that become lost time paper shuffling and that can be put to better use. Find those minutes that make up the time you need to put into this new business model. When it comes to online work, you are your own boss. So state how many hours you are willing to invest and are going to be putting in to your success. Write this down and commit to it.

Schedule your day and live your day to your schedule to get the most hourly benefits.

Say you attend to day as such: Arrive at your office by 8:30am, get lunch by 1:00pm, schedule in one hour for rest and a few errands. By 5:30pm have your dinner and family time until perhaps 9:30pm to 10:00pm, from 10pm to 12am this is your time for extracurricular projects. Perhaps this is the time for those projects that are not your heavy money makers but are for personal development. This might be your study time and time to clean up some pending tasks (finish up a blog page, an article, prepare the press release)

Break up your activities so that you can schedule some evenings as training time to go through your back office media vault or whatever your program's back office provides. Make it a point to learn and to apply the materials. And if your program does not provide a decent back office for training, perhaps you are in the wrong program! My signature line directs you to review a back office full of training- a real handful and definitely more than your money's worth!

Treat your business as a business. Also treat your venture as if it were your first job and never ever tell yourself no. Would you tell your boss no?

Remember the old saying, "Pay yourself first?" Well, this is true whether you are talking about saving for retirement or preparing a new retirement cash flow solution using the internet as your vehicle to making money while working from home.

Set schedules and goals. Do this for one month as a commitment. After that month, I assure you that you will have found a tremendous increase in your productivity.

Write out tomorrow's schedule at night before you go to bed. Include the most important things that you must get done by tomorrow.

For example, schedule yourself to write one article, read some books, watch three training videos. Whatever you want to accomplish and make it a goal that you can't go to bed without getting these six things done.

Email is a real time waster for many of us. Set aside 20-30 minutes for email responses. And remember, this is not for fun. This will rob you of precious minutes that you could be tasking money-making little projects, like articles and blogs that go out into the internet as faithful soldiers looking for your prospects.

One hour every day for education, one hour for implementing what you learned to day before) at least partially). Write down your questions, and then go to Google.

Keep a success journal, your goals for the day, the goals accomplished, and log what's going on in your head and the new ideas you get each day. Have this mental journal on paper so that you can leave the breadcrumbs of your education behind in a time line that you can go back and review, or tweak in the near future. This is a wonderful ruler by which to gauge how far you've come in your online business over time.

Create and live by your schedule, and your productivity will go through the roof.

Secondly, get into your goals. Your brain works on this list that you create for yourself during the night and sets you up for success the following day.

Therefore, these good habits send a message to your subconscious regarding the goals you have willed yourself to achieve and gives you the confidence to continue as you document each goal that you have completed.

Rinse and repeat every day.

After a while your goals start getting bigger and your subconscious tells you that you can get it done because it builds on your accomplishments. Therefore, the smaller tasks are like rungs that start you climbing that ladder of success that you have placed for yourself.

Goals are many and diverse. See yourself as a living, global entity and schedule your personal goals, physical goals, health goals, family goals, financial goals, business goals. Go hog wild with this and see yourself excel in more areas than you ever thought possible in one lifetime. Begin to expand from your personal goals for accomplishment into your social and spiritual goals, think in terms of your roles in society, with your friends and your community.

Remember, you are a multi-dimensional divine blessing to this world. You have been given the power to excel beyond your wildest imagination. You dictate your life and only you can determine where you end up. It's in the thoughts and the beliefs that you hold in your heart and deep within your subconscious mind.

But, back to the more immediate time line. Start small; after all, this may be a new way of looking at your life for you. This may be a new start at learning the art of discipline and control.

Start with your short term goals. What will you accomplish in a daily, weekly, monthly or perhaps even quarterly schedule? Then move into your medium and longer range goals. Say, where would you want to be within the next 5 years, or so.

Always remember, in five years you will always be 5 years older, but why not also be richer, smarter, financially liberated, earning passive and residual income having broken out of the selling 'time for money' mindset that keeps people from pursuing their loftier goals. What the heck, it's the same five years, right?

Make it happen for yourself and then look over your shoulder and say, "Wow, look how far I have traveled, one step and one day at a time."

Here Are Your Brainstorm Questions:

- What is it that you really want?
- Why is it that you want it?
- Do you have the fire in your belly to get it?
- What will it do for you?
- When will you reach it?
- What is your time frame for achieving this?
- What are you going to give in return for this goal?

After you chew on this, write out a clear goal and a complete statement of the synopsis of these answers.

Don't be flip about it. Write everything out clearly and concisely and put it on many 3x5 cards where you can read them every day and night.. Feel it and see it as being done.

These are success habits that once implemented twill makes you far more productive as you focus on what it is that you really want in your life.

Connect With Your Partners

Your partner must not be neglected by your lifestyle. During the day, you consume most – if not all – of your energy during working hours. After which, you dream of nothing more than going to bed. This might bother your partner after a while.

However, you can treat your spouse nicely (if you know what I mean) by waking him or her up "the right way". What better way to start the day other than having an intimate time with your significant other?

People who understand cause and effect will also understand how to achieve success in business. I've coached people in their businesses and in their personal relationships in learning to connect on an emotional level with their customers and their families. I assist them in understanding how is money generated in their business; who is it they need to be building relationships with; what are the constraints holding them back; and how they connect emotionally is vital to the cause and effect of success.

Successful people in the top 10% have different thoughts than most. They think about what they want and how to get it, and they think about what others want and how they can help them get it. Successful people know how to build relationships but they had to learn it just like you and I.

If you trace back to find out how someone achieved success in business then you will find cause and effect in place. You can put your feet in their tracks to find out how they started from nothing and became wealthy, and if you followed their path then you too can create wealth.

Unsuccessful people think about what they don't have, why they don't have it, which's to blame, and why they can never get it, consequently all of their relationships suffer.

Your job is to think about what you want and how to get it, whether in business or in your family life. If you want a wonderful relationship with your partners or your family then you will think about how you can achieve it. You will search for better ways until your relationships blossom.

When you ask the 'how' instead of why, the 'how' brings you into taking complete responsibility of your life, it gives you complete confidence, you become the action taker, a person of self-control.

Did you hear me say your spouse needs to get off the couch and take action? Did you hear me say your business partner needs to learn to run a better business? No, cause and effect takes shape within you understand first, not your spouse or partner. I often say, "Be the hero you want your spouse to be" and you'll see change.

Make it a reality for your life. This may sound cliché' but what matters is where you are going, not where you are right now or where you have been. If you are not continuing your education where relationships are concerned then you are not growing, nor taking responsibility.

You can always tell who a person is by what they do because what they do is a true expression of their core values. Only action equals action toward success.

One of the kindest things you could do for any one is to share your ideas on how to be successful in relationships, in business or in life with others. You will build the relationships you want by giving, or bringing increase, into those you are seeking relationships from. Again, try it consistently for 10 days and see what happens.

Two Questions to ask yourself: How hard are you willing to work to keep the weeds away? How willing are you to cultivate your business and family relationships?

My personal belief is one of the greatest gifts ever given to us by the creator was the Gift of Relationships.

Learn Something New

You should never stop learning. No matter how much you know there is always room for more information. Just as science discovers that the more that we figure out about the world around us in the universe the more we realize that we don't know; It works the same way with your learning as well. Spend a little time each and every day learning something new that is going to help you. You could read a motivational book.

There are many different ones out there that are geared towards entrepreneurs and are written to give great advice from experts who actually have made a success out of entrepreneurship. You can find them at your local library or online in digital format. Books by Anthony Robbins, Stephen R. Covey, Dale Carnegie and Napoleon Hill are all great reads if you're trying to motivate yourself and become more successful. There are many other places that you can find motivation.

Go on YouTube during your free time and look for motivational videos if that's more your style or you could even correspond via email with someone who is more successful than you who could be your mentor of sorts. No matter how you get information the point is to keep learning and to devote some time each day to that learning. You don't even necessarily have to read motivational or self-help books. You could do something that improves yourself like learning a new language or teaching yourself a new skill, or by studying a subject that you been interested in, relating to your business.

Mark Fisher, CEO and Founder of Assignment Masters, suggests that:

"It lies in our human nature to learn something new every day. Nevertheless, a successful person doesn't wait for it to happen. He wants to be one step ahead, and he craves success like he craves air to breathe. Because of this need for growth, it would be best if you'd start your morning by feeding your brain with educational material.

Any self-respecting goal setter knows that achieving a goal will inevitably involve learning new skills. No matter what you set out to do, you will have to gain new capabilities and new understanding about yourself along the way.

Expanding your personal skill set is a big part of the pleasure and the challenge of being an effective goal setter, which is why it makes perfect sense to include a learning target in your everyday planning. Here is why self-education should be part of your daily ritual and how to ensure that it is.

Keep your mind fresh. As a child, your earliest years were the period when your mind expanded at its fastest rate as you continuously absorbed new and fascinating information about the world. This process slows as we grow older, but if it stops altogether we become dull and staid. Our brains are naturally curious and to stay fresh and alert they need constant new stimulus. Research shows that continuous learning helps to stave off problems like Alzheimers in our later years.

Plan it into your day. As a goal setter you will already be skilled at writing down your daily tasks and disciplined at getting through them efficiently. My advice is to add an extra element to your day plan and challenge yourself to take on board new knowledge, as well as complete the tasks you set yourself.

Learn one new thing a day. So as not to get overloaded, I suggest you keep the learning curve down to a manageable level, so one a day is perfectly acceptable. The key thing is that the skill you learn should be in line with your goal. For example, if you are trying to build your first website, then learning a new knitting stitch, might be fun, but is not going to bring you closer to your aims. However, learning one new feature of HTML each day, or reading one more chapter in your Dreamweaver manual makes much more sense.

At the end of each day, look back and be proud of what you have learned. Keep a journal of new skills and at the end of the year you will be staggered by the new capabilities you have mastered.

Pick one, two at the most. You may like all of these ideas. That's fine, but you have to pick. Perhaps you will try two each day (some can be done in less than 30 minutes), or perhaps you will do one during the week and another on the weekends.

Find what works best for you.

And start today (or tomorrow morning, at the latest).

TRAITS OF HIGHLY SUCCESSFUL PEOPLE

In this world, we, as individuals, have lots of aspirations and dreams. Throughout the stage of growing up, we tend to idealize key people in our life, who can either be our favorite movie stars, sportsmen, teachers, family members or even politicians. This gradual idealism leaves an impact on us and at times, our personality reflects certain traits of our ideals which we have absorbed from them in the due course of time.

To say that hard work alone is the key to success is not entirely true. Though working hard will bring people to improvement, there are other traits that are proven to be effective ingredients to reaching success. It does not matter what field the person is in. Whether it's in business, a career, a profession, or scientific discoveries and inventions, all of the successful people in these areas did not rely on hard work alone. So, you may think, how were these successful men and women as people, before they reached their goals? What common traits did they have that we could all possibly learn from so that we too can become someone and accomplish bigger things too? Success always leaves clues and by modeling successful people we can find success in our own lives.

All the great pioneers, entrepreneurs and entertainers of the world possess certain characteristics that have seen them achieve incredible success. But the good news is, these are success traits not just afforded to an exclusive group of people. They are not things that they were born with.

They are things that can be easily developed by you, me and everyone else, if the drive and desire for success is strong.

Everyone has an entitlement to be successful, but as you probably know by now, success is not something that just happens.

So is there actually certain criterion for idealizing people in our life? Should we randomly idealize just anybody who inspires us? Well, the thing is, that not all individuals are worthy of idealism. It also depends upon how, we, as a person, would want to see ourselves. A thief would always idealize his mafia leader, not the local priest! So, if we aspire to be worthy and successful individuals, then we need to idealize people who have the following important traits:

Ambition

To be successful, you need ambition. Ambitious people will see that they are capable of doing their best and being the best and what they do. If you feel that you are not good enough, or not capable, then you can be unlikely to try and reach your goals of success.

If you can believe in yourself and try your best, you can become a lot more ambitious. Having a strong desire to succeed is part of the journey to actually succeeding. If you know what you want to achieve, and you have the determination to go for it; this can really help you.

Courage

A lot of the time, most people do not achieve success because of fear. Many people have a fear of failing and this is what can stop them from achieving. Some of the most successful people will say that failing is key to succeeding and that you need to make mistakes. Having this mindset is a quality required for success.

If you have courage, you can stop being so fearful of failing and instead, focus on what you can achieve. If you can look at mistakes and failures as lessons to learn from, this can also encourage you to keep going and try to succeed.

Courage is a great trait to have if you want to be successful. It will help you to develop the right mindset when it comes to reaching your goals and you won't be afraid to try, even after you make a mistake.

Commitment

When someone is committed, they will have the determination to achieve what they want and will keep trying to reach that goal. Success and commitment go hand in hand! Most successful people will believe in themselves and their goals for success, they will become committed to achieving it.

When you believe in what you are trying to succeed, you believe in yourself and what you can do. Therefore, you are very likely to become committed to proving to yourself that you can succeed. People who are not committed will find this very hard as they could lose focus on their goals and give up before they reach success.

Willpower

Willpower is a great trait to have, especially if you want to succeed in life. Those who have great willpower can focus and strive for their goals, solely focusing on achieving. When you have a lot of willpower, you are less likely to procrastinate or make excuses, because you will be determined to succeed.

If you have no willpower, you are more likely to give up easily or change what you are doing, as procrastination can become more prominent and you may lose interest in trying to achieve your goals.

Integrity

In order to succeed, integrity is an important trait to have. When you are honest, people will believe in you, they can help you and you can also take pride in knowing that you are honest with yourself and others.

Not only is this just a good trait to have in general, it will help you to become more successful too! Integrity can help to define who you are and how you act towards others. This can help you on your journey to success. If you are honest and have good morals, then you can trust yourself and your own success.

Drive

Having the drive and determination to work harder, to keep going and try new things, is an excellent trait to have when it comes to being successful. Without drive, you are not going to be as passionate about what you are trying to achieve, therefore you are more unlikely to achieve it.

Make sure that you can stay determined and passionate about what it is you want to succeed in so that you have a constant drive to succeed.

Patience

If you can be more patient, this can really help you when trying to be successful. Patience will help you when it comes to making any mistakes or having to deal with problems on your journey to success.

If you have little, or no patience, this is going to make things much harder for you. You will not be able to deal with the obstacles very well! Understanding that things take time, and unfortunately, mistakes can be made, is crucial. You could become successful much quicker if you can accept this!

Optimism

If you are an optimist, it's likely that you will be excited about what you are trying to achieve, and feel good about it too. Having an optimistic attitude is a great trait to have if you want to be successful, as it can help you to stay positive about what you are doing, and not be disheartened if things go wrong.

Being optimistic can really help you because you will believe those good things can happen! You would expect positive outcomes to come from your journey to success too.

Resilience

Even if you get knocked down at the first hurdle, you should always keep going. Resilience is a key trait for success as it is what can help you to continue going, no matter what. In life, you will face obstacles and things that might hinder your success. However, having resilience can really help you to bounce back from these things quickly.

If you are not resilient, you may run away as soon as you have to face a difficult situation, which will not help you on your journey to becoming successful. Try and become more resilient. Learn to deal with tough situations, so that you can power through and become successful.

Actually knowing and believing that you have the power to succeed can be difficult, but it's something that can really benefit you. We all have the ability to succeed in life and get what we want! We just need to know how to reach our full potential.

CONCLUSION

One of the biggest mistakes you can make as a professional seeking to achieve in your field is to disregard the importance of a positive attitude. Time and time again I have heard positive attitude described as a "soft skill," but the reality is that most of the dysfunction in business and personal achievement can be traced back to the root cause of - you guessed it - negative, ineffective thinking habits.

The world famous coach Tony Robbins has been using what he calls "incantation" for decade's right before meeting a client or holding a seminar. He uses both his body and words to put himself in the right state and reach a level of perfect certainty. There are many times when I wish I could use those incantations but it is not easy to shout in public places or in the toilets before an event.

Obstacles are part of the life plan. The Road of Life is not a straight road. It is filled with potholes, construction zones, detours and things to get in your way. Your attitude will play a big part in this, as it has to be positive enough to keep you on the path to success in whatever area you are working on. If obstacles present themselves, go around them, over them, through them. Don't let any obstacle get in the way of your pursuit of success and happiness.

If you understood the term homeostasis, you now realize how hard it is to create positive change without a solid game plan and strategy. By nature we don't like change.

Be enthusiastic! Enthusiasm fuels progress - it is the prime method of persuasion without pressure. The more enthusiasm you have the better. Enthusiasm is a magic spark that breeds success in everyone within its radius.

Be considerate of others. Be dependable. Take pride in your work, whatever it may be. As it says in the Desiderata - it is a real possession in the changing fortunes of time.

Try to see the good in all things no matter how mundane they seem to be.

But sometimes, we let ourselves get bogged down with negativity. What can we do to get rid of any negative attitudes we might have?

Believe in yourself. You are unique in this world - and so are your talents. The real secret of a successful person is the absolute confidence they have in themselves and their abilities. Enter every activity without giving mental recognition to the possibility of defeat. Concentrate on your strengths instead of your weaknesses. A positive mental attitude is rooted in clear, calm and honest self-confidence.

Care about other people. There's no better example of a positive attitude than the Golden Rule. That is, treat people the same way you want to be treated.

Get fun out of life. Don't take yourself too seriously. Laugh and the world laughs with you - cry and you cry alone. Studies have proven that when we laugh, there is an actual chemical change in our bodies that helps to ease pain and release stress. Laughter is a coping mechanism for the normal stress of life.

Be so strong that nothing can disturb your peace of mind. Look at the sunny side of everything, and make your optimism come true. Give so much time to the improvement of yourself that you have no time to criticize others. Forget the mistakes of the past and press on to greater achievement in the future. Be too big for worry, too noble for anger, too strong for fear, and too happy to permit the presence of trouble to invade your beautiful personality.

I leave you with these wise words. The author is anonymous.

"Today I can complain about my health.
Or I can celebrate being alive.
Today I can moan that it is raining,
Or be joyful at all that grows from the rain.

Today I can regret all that I don't have

Or rejoice in everything I do have.

Today I can mourn everything I have lost,

Or eagerly anticipate what's to come.

Today I can complain that I have to work,

Or celebrate having a job to go to.

Today I can resent the mess the kids make,

Or give thanks that I have a family.

Today I can whine about the housework,

Or celebrate having a home.

Today I can cry over the people who don't care for me, Or be happy, loving and being loved by those who do."

So the question is: what shall I choose for today? Again, a positive attitude is a personal choice. Tomorrow I will have a great day because I choose to have a great attitude.

What kind of day will YOU have?
Smile. The choice is yours.

Do not go yet; One last thing to do

If you enjoyed this book or found it useful I'd be very grateful if you'd post a short review on **Amazon**. Your support really does make a difference and I read all the reviews personally so I can get your feedback and make this book even better.

Thanks again for your support!